THE ELEPHANT'S PEACEABLE KINGDOM

AND OTHER SALTY FABLES

THE ELEPHANT'S PEACEABLE KINGDOM

AND OTHER SALTY FABLES

by Nathan Cabot Hale
with illustrations by the author

Foreword by
GERARD PIEL

An appreciation by
DONALD HOLDEN

White Whale Press • New York

Library of Congress
Catalog Card Number:

ISBN   0-9640029-1-4

Published by White Whale Press
Amenia, N.Y.

Printed and bound in the
United States of America

Dedicated to my grandchildren,
Amy, Max and Maya.

ACKNOWLEDGEMENTS

To my wife Alison for her loving patience and for
    checking my errors.
To Joan Laurie Poole, poet and editor, for her
    masterful editing.
To Maureen Rooney for overseeing the
    production of this book.
To Cathy Wing for her skills in typography and
    layout.
Thank you ladies!

FOREWORD

Visitors to the Elephant's Peaceable Kingdom will not meet any of the animals they remember from Aesop. Here they are altogether contemporary — the utopian elephant, to begin with, a bulimic fox and similarly troubled rhinoceros, a fundamentalist bookworm, a Forbes-400 wolf and a brace of other get-rich-quick promoters, fundamentalist preachers, faith healers, excretory exhibitionists, sexual athletes, three culinary witches, a fraudulent cosmologist, and a narcissistic hoyden or two. Noah's Ark would have foundered in the Flood, had it been burdened with the essential two of each of these creatures. They would not be here to tell their tales.

That raises the question of how they got here. The four millennia of the Judeo-Christian era are a long time. That is not time enough, however, to bring to perfection by natural selection the departures in animal behavior to be observed in the Elephant's Peaceable Kingdom. Not Noah's nor Aesop's menagerie could have undergone such transformation in so short a time.

Only one mode of evolution proceeds at this velocity. That is social evolution. Its mode is Lamarckian; that is, learning and experience are conveyed, by precept and example, in the genetic heritage to the next generation.

Here is the clue that answers the question. The animals of this not so peaceable kingdom are the social animal. In recoil from the inward frailty, insipidity, salacity, cupidity, duplicity and general iniquity, so intolerably manifested in outward behavior, he (she) falls into the error of anthropomorphism. She (he) attributes such manifestation to other animals, made thus invidiously lower. It is not man, for example, but the ape in man.

Anthropomorphism can be seen thus to be one of the many cruelties of man to beast. Nor does it pay any compliment when it is more innocently invoked as the pathetic fallacy in lame (lame-brained) explanation of animal behavior by the attribution of a human faculty or capacity.

Here, in the Elephant's Peaceable Kingdom, Nathan Cabot Hale has stood anthropomorphism on its head. The animals re-enact faithfully, at times poignantly, and, when appropriate, hilariously the all too practiced routines of the cerebral vertebrate that has appointed itself as the, from now on, in-charge of evolution. What is more they — well, almost all of them — have a great time doing so.

For bonus, the artist-author has thrown in a Just So story that Rudyard Kipling would have wished he had thought of: How the Batrachian Camel Got His Two Humps.

Gerard Piel

NATHAN CABOT HALE
AN APPRECIATION

Nathan Cabot Hale has been my friend for over thirty years — and he still surprises me by the range of his talents and his interests.

Long before I met Nathan, I'd admired his sculpture at New York's Midtown Galleries. His figures radiated a profound knowledge of the human form and were modeled with such vitality and fluidity that I was astonished to discover that they were welded— "modeled" with the welding torch. I found the figures so beautiful and the craftsmanship so remarkable that I asked Nathan to write a book for Watson-Guptill Publications, a publisher of books for artists and art students, where I served as Editorial Director.

The result was <u>Welded Sculpture,</u> not only the best book on the technique of welding for the sculptor, but one of the most inspiring art instruction books I'd ever seen. <u>Welded Sculpture</u> remains the best book on the subject.

Nathan then turned from art instruction to art history and produced one of the classic books in the literature of sculpture, <u>Embrace of Life: The Sculpture of Gustave Vigeland</u>. The text (with superb photographs by David Finn) not only paid tribute to the great Norwegian sculptor, but enriched my appreciation of the sculpture and advanced Nathan's passionate belief that the essential subject of figure sculpture is the cycle of life. The Vigeland book is treasured by sculptors around the world.

Nathan's next book, also published by Watson-Guptill when I worked there, was an extraordinary intellectual achievement: <u>Abstraction in Art and Nature.</u> In text, drawings, and photographs, he explored the logic and the consistency of nature's "designs" from the galaxy to earth forms, plants, animals, and the human species. The book is a treasure house of insights and ideas for working artists, designers, and craftsmen. Another classic.

Always fascinated by the natural sciences and psychology, Nathan turned from writing about art to writing about human behavior. The result was a poetic and deeply moving book about the role of the father in natural childbirth: <u>The Birth of a Family</u>.

Having read Nathan's prose over the years, I confess that I wasn't surprised to receive his lovely volume of poems, <u>Fox Tails</u>. What I love about these poems is that I can hear Nathan's voice — the sounds and rhythms of that voice — meditating on all the issues that have fascinated him throughout his life. There are memorable poems about seeing and knowing, about living creatures, about the cosmos, about our origins in the water. As a painter obsessed with water, I love the lines:

> A reflected universe I see...
> Light collected by the lens...
> In a medium of water in a darkened pool...

And now this delightful book of fables for grownups — well, for alleged grownups. Nathan's fables are full of sardonic wit, the zany humor that he usually reserves for conversation, and the sort of laughter that Byron meant when he said: "I laugh only that I may not weep." Like all really good fables, Nathan's cautionary tales make you laugh and make you uneasy at the same time. The fables are about you, of course. And about me. The delicious drawings also make me wish that Nathan had pursued one more career as an illustrator of children's books.

The list of Nathan Cabot Hale's achievements goes on and on. A lifetime commitment to sculpture, of course. But also painting, drawing, prose, poetry, art instruction, art history, art criticism, research into the natural and behavioral sciences. Nathan has a restless and passionate mind. I think he may be surprised when I add that he is — in his own way — a devout man. He reminds me of William Blake, who said: "Everything that lives is holy."

Donald Holden
Irvington-on-Hudson, NY

TABLE OF CONTENTS

SOME INTRODUCTORY THOUGHTS
ON THE ORIGINS AND USE OF FABLES

Fables have been a part of human lore since the days when people gathered around the fire at the cave mouth to spin yarns of the past, and prognostications of the future. The creatures of the world have been our fascinating companions since the beginning of time. But for the last ten thousand years or so, our feelings have wavered between our sense of natural reverence for our fellow creatures (the Egyptian animal Gods of nature for example), and the haughty belief that we are far above these lowly beasts. Yet underneath it all, there has remained a deep subconscious knowledge that these "others" are our brethren. The problem has been whether we should deny our obvious kinship to save our egos, or to submerge ourselves in the mystical knowledge that our spirits are intertwined with the often frightening animal world. This confused wavering continued until a couple of centuries ago when science began to unravel the true meanings of our biological relationships with all life.

If we go far enough back into the murky depths of evolution, we find that all life originated with the single cell, and that actually a great depth of kinship exists between all living creatures. So we find that the traits of vertebrate animal behavior are akin to our own human animal traits. And I believe that this is the reason why animal fables work so well for human moral instruction. Animal fables allow us to see our faults of character with a much kinder eye, for the fable allows us to learn from these imaginary fellow creatures...without the painful sting of direct human reference.

I believe though, that many people have accepted the validity of evolutionary theory, but have not yet fully realized the depth of meaning in these concepts. For this reason, it is good to think about how we conceptualize human character traits by comparing them with our vertebrate brothers...the animals. We can find rich behavioral analogies in the traits of many of our fellow creatures... even in those of birds, and the occasional insect... for all living creatures seek food, and sex, and love just as we do... proving the inherent similarities that unite all animal life.

In this present book of fables I have used the writer's trick of displacing human emotions onto the persons of the animals... so that the fictional animal creatures are made to act as if they were humans. This is a useful device that writers sometimes use to show the shortcomings of humans with a greater objective distance and clarity, and... possibly... with a greater sense of preposterous amusement. We know that animals don't behave in such absurd ways, but this enables us to say that certain people appear to act like the fictional elephant, the bear, the fox, or even the cockroach. The thing is, because of our innate humanity, we always hope that humans will really behave a little better than they do, with more personal awareness, with a little less ego, and yes, with a little less emotional density.

So, though the writer of these fables may have used his animal subjects a bit unjustly in order to show the foibles of humans... deep down, beneath all his artifice... he loves his fellow animals and feels a deep and abiding respect for them. He knows that animals would never act as foolishly as the characters he has described in his fables. So he apologizes to the greater animal world for the liberties that he has taken with many of its wonderful citizens.

With these thoughts I commend these tales to you.

Nathan Cabot Hale
Amenia, NY

The Elephant's
Peaceable Kingdom

A retired elephant who was well off (he had saved his brass and made his pile) was at odds as to what to do with his money. After considerable thought, he decided to form a utopian community based on the highest ethical principles, a place where all animals could live together in peace and harmony. He determined to call his community "The Peaceable Kingdom," and he advertised in all the newspapers to tell the creatures of his plans for a perfect life. The advert ran as follows:

ATTENTION!

ALL CREATURES INTERESTED
JOINING UTOPIAN COMMUNITY
(VEGETARIAN PRINCIPLES)
FOR BROTHERHOOD, EQUALITY,
SEE THE ELEPHANT.
9 A.M. - 5 P.M.

The first to answer were a lion and a fox. They told the elephant that they had long been searching for a better way of life, and they volunteered to help him find converts for his Peaceable Kingdom — the lion to contact the larger creatures and the fox to recruit the smaller ones. The elephant was as pleased as he could be. It was decided that he would give a big garden party to bring all of the interested parties together.

The garden party was a huge success, and many recruits for the utopian community were made. The lion recruited a gazelle, a cow, two sheep, a nanny goat, and an ostrich. The fox brought in a dozen chickens, five rabbits, a turkey, three lambs, and a dozen squirrels. The elephant was even more pleased, and without further ado he settled them all on a ten acre plot that he had set aside on his estate for the project. And since the lion and the fox had been the first to join the Peaceable Kingdom, he decided to give them the administrative duties of the community. Having complete faith in these new assistants, he promised to look in later in the month, after all the members had settled in, to check how they were all getting along.

Things went on, the world turned, the stock market rose and fell, the flowers bloomed, and when the day for the elephant's visit arrived, he entered the grounds of the Peaceable Kingdom to find them quite deserted except for the lion and the fox, who were sitting at a table eating the remains of what appeared to be a roast turkey.

"What's going on here?" sputtered the disgruntled elephant. "Where are all my utopians?"

"We've run into a spot of difficulty." replied the fox, brandishing a roast turkey leg, "The lion and I have found it very hard to convert to vegetarianism all at one go. The fact is, we were just about ready to look you up to see about advertising for some more recruits. We're really working on this vegetarian thing and think we'll have it down pat in a few more weeks."

The astounded elephant immediately ordered the fox and the lion off his property and closed the gates of the Peaceable Kingdom forever.

"That was a wonderful utopia," said the fox as the two were leaving. "I just dearly love a utopia."

"Champion," replied the lion picking his teeth, "absolutely champion!"

Moral: Utopias generally work till the vittles run out.

The Last Lion

On the day the last lion died, a fly flew into the nose of the dead body and laid some eggs. A few days thereafter, the maggots began to hatch and eagerly eat their way through the corpse. As the maggots slowly became conscious of themselves and their fellows, they began to wonder about the nature of life. They stopped eating. They pondered fate. But finally one maggot, the one that was first to hatch, saw that they were getting thinner. He told his fellows that if they would resume eating the lions flesh, they would surely eventually come on the Portal of Salvation. And all went well for a time...until they questioned who they were.

"But what are we?" the maggots asked in unison.

"We are a lion," the leader replied.

This seemed to satisfy them until they had eaten their way to the other end of the lion, and there before them was a portal through which they could see the sun shining. They shouted in amazement and all of them rushed to the light crying, "The Portal of Salvation!" But an unusual thing happened, as they rushed toward the light, they were overcome by strange feelings as they suddenly burst out of their skins and metamorphosed into flies.

The newly hatched flies flew out of the Portal of Salvation and swarmed above the now dried out carcass of the last lion. And there, again terrified by the open air and the sunlight, they begged their leader for some explanation of their existence.

"What are we?" cried the newly hatched flies.

The new leader, the first to hatch and the first to fly from the Portal of Salvation, replied with considerable pride as he looked at the lion's carcass below them, "We are the risen soul of the last lion!"

Moral: A dead lion is much easier to eat than a live one.

The Case of The Fat Fox

A fox who suffered from obesity consulted a famous owl who practiced psychiatry. The fox's case history revealed that he lived near a barn loaded with grain, which was infested with mice. Because of the plethora of mice, the fox no longer had to hunt for his meals, but would merely station himself by a mouse hole and gorge himself to his heart's content.

"I just don't feel like my old self anymore," the fox complained to the owl. "Life doesn't have the zip for me that it used to have."

"You are suffering a very serious depression," said the owl gravely. "I believe that psychotherapeutic treatment might be beneficial for your condition. We must seek out the roots of your eating compulsion. I suggest that you come for treatment an hour each day, five days a week. The charge will be twenty mice per session."

The fat fox agreed to come to the owl for therapy and began to catch twenty extra mice a day for the owl's fee. The extra movement and exertion caused the fox to feel a bit more lively than he had before. "This treatment seems to be doing me good," he said to himself. "What a fine psychiatrist that owl is!" And he settled into the daily sessions with growing confidence.

However, after a month of treatment, the owl announced to the fox that, due to inflation, his fee would have to be raised to forty mice per session. The fox agreed to this, but the doubling of the fee required him to exert more energy to feed himself and catch the required number of mice to pay the owl. As a result of this increased effort, his weight began to stabilize and he became even more active. Zest began to return to his life. He started to take walks with his wife and even went possum hunting in the evenings with his friends. This increased activity led to a systematic process of weight loss.

"I feel wonderful doctor," he told the owl. "I feel ten years younger!"

Hearing this the owl looked grave and told the fox that the therapy was reaching down to the basic level of health that had been buried in the deeper layers of the fox's subconscious. However, he added that mounting inflation necessitated a further raising of his fee to sixty mice per session, to which the fox readily agreed.

To fill the owl's new quota of sixty mice per day and still feed himself, the fox had to exert his full energy and talent. Under this new regimen, he soon returned to his normal weight. The owl, on the other hand, had become so fat that he fell off a limb and broke his neck. A great funeral was held for the owl and scholars and savants from all over the country came to pay tribute to the their departed colleague. The fox mourned his lost physician, but by that time he had lost his taste for mice and was able to maintain his renewed sleek form through the vigorous pursuit of possum. But he often stopped to silently pay tribute to the memory of the great healer.

Moral: Mother Nature gives life, but she is also a marvelous executioner.

The Bookworm
and The Bible

In the library of a great bibliophile there lived a studious bookworm. One day this bookworm was making his way among the precious volumes when he suddenly realized that it was long past his lunch. "I'm terribly hungry," he said. "I would dearly love some Omar Khayyam!" But since he remembered that the Rubiayat was all the way at the other end of the library, he realized that he would have to dine on something else. Right at that very moment, he saw a King James version of the Holy Bible before him. "I think I'll try some of that," he said as he made his way into Genesis. And being very hungry indeed and finding the book to his liking, he ate his way right through to Revelation.

Emerging from the good book, the bookworm happened to encounter an old friend who greeted him by saying, "I see you're into religion these days."

"Yes indeed and very good it is," replied the bookworm. "I particularly enjoyed passages through Deuteronomy, Ephesians, and Jude, but I must confess that I found Leviticus, Habakkuk, and Galatians rather dry going."

"You seem to be quite an authority on the book," said the bookworm's friend.

"Yes, indeed," answered the bookworm, "I've thoroughly digested the entire work."

"You said a mouthful," replied his friend, "you speak volumes."

"How true," replied the bookworm, "Praise the Lord!"

Moral: God speaks to all creatures in their own language.

The Constipated Rhinoceros

In the far regions of the African veldt there was once a rhinoceros who had a compulsive eating habit and was seriously constipated. He would sometimes strain for days in the hope of relieving himself. Sometimes it would take a month for him to achieve success.

One day after great effort, the rhinoceros managed to pass a hard rectangular object that looked just like a brick. The entire process had been observed by an entrepreneurial hyena.

"Say, that looks just like a brick," said the hyena. "Can you do that every time?"

"Yes," replied the rhino sadly, "its like that every single time."

"Howsabout you an me goin inta business," said the hyena, seeing limitless possibilities. "We could make a fortune sellin these things to the contractors in the building trades. You make 'em and I'll peddle 'em to the industry."

So the rhinoceros and the hyena signed a partnership agreement, and the hyena began to solicit orders. But after several weeks, the hyena returned to find that the rhinoceros had produced no bricks at all. It seemed that the thought of making money had so cheered the rhinoceros that his intestinal blockage had cleared and all that he produced were the fluffy round turds that all the other herbivores produced, and they had no structural integrity whatever! So in anger the hyena dissolved the partnership and went forth to seek new business opportunities leaving the rhinoceros to live a contented and more temperate life.

Moral: Certain kinds of success ain't worth the effort.

The Pig of
The Golden West

Once there was a pig who had dreams of being a real cowboy. This pig lived in a big city and worked in a restaurant as a fry cook. But at night the pig would watch western movies on TV and would then practice playing his guitar and singing cowboy songs. On weekends he practiced the art of walking in cowboy boots, sometimes he would saunter, at other times he would practice moseying. When the time came that he felt he had mastered all the arts of the west, the pig quit his job at the restaurant and bought a bus ticket to Montana.

When the bus finally got to Montana, the eager pig asked the driver to let him off at the first really big cattle ranch. So the driver dropped the pig off where a dusty road joined the highway and he told the pig to walk up the road to the end where he'd find the biggest ranch in the state. The pig thanked the driver, shouldered his bedroll, and walked up the road to the ranch where he found a cowboy sitting on a fence looking at a horse in the corral.

"Howdy pardner," said the cowboy. "What can I do fer ya?"

"Lookin' fer the ramrod," said the pig.

"Yer lookin' at 'im," replied the cowboy. "What's up?"

"Lookin' fer work," said the pig.

"What kind?" asked the ramrod.

"Cowboyin'" said the pig.

"What can ya do?" asked the ramrod.

"Oh, jist about everthin," said the pig. "I can spit, cuss, walk bowlegged, spin my roscoe, do-si-do, play my geetar, look threatnin, hunker down, and talk real growly."

"Kin ya ride that bronc?" asked the ramrod, pointing to the horse in the corral.

"The horse ain't been borned can throw me!" replied the pig.

"Didn't think so," replied the ramrod. "Lemme saddle this old nag up so yu kin do yer stuff." He thereupon saddled the horse and helped the pig mount the bronc. A moment or two later, he went to help the pig up off the ground.

"Whassa matter with yer leg?" asked the ramrod.

"I think its busted." said the pig.

"Thought so," said the ramrod. "Yu wait right here while I phone fer the ammalance."

Two months later, the pig limped up the same road to find the ramrod still sitting on the same fence.

"What can I do fer ya pardner?" asked the ramrod.

"I'm jist a stove up old bronc rider lookin' fer work," said the pig.

"What kind?" asked the ramrod.

"I'm a cookin' fool," replied the pig. "Freeholies with sidemeat's ma speshulty, follered close by chicken fried steak."

The ramrod hired the pig on the spot.

The pig became an institution in the area. The cowboys all loved his freeholies and his geetar playing. And the tourists who visited from the big city all thought he was the saltiest old cowpoke of the lot. They loved to have him pose for photographs in his regalia.

Moral: When simulated authenticity don't work, try some genyoowine ersatz.

The Doomsday Wolf

A reprehensible wolf had cheated, manipulated, connived, betrayed, tricked, and stolen from everyone he had ever met. And what was even worse, he slandered and blamed the very people he had tricked and betrayed for having all the loathsome traits he had himself. He was completely rotten, but he was also very rich. And as a result of all of these qualities of his character, he was invited to the parties everywhere and all of the creatures talked about how wonderful he was...when he was near. But when he was not near, they were afraid of him because they understood that he was heartless.

The reprehensible wolf had nothing but contempt for the other creatures, even though they always invited him to their parties and always flattered him to his face. He saw that behind their eyes they were afraid of him and his heartlessness. When he thought about their fear, he would laugh to himself and say, "I'm all wolf and a yard wide!"

But one day as the wolf was walking in the gardens of his great estate and admiring the roses, he felt a jolt of strange dread shake his body. He felt that something terrible was going to happen! He began to tremble and he ran into his great house and up the great stairway and down the long hall to his bedroom, where he locked the door and hid in the closet till his trembling ceased. The following morning he looked at his face in the mirror over his wash stand and saw that his eyes had circles under them and his forehead had a worried look. "I am all wolf and a yard wide," he cried to himself, "I am the one who has always made the other creatures worry, but now something is making me worry!"

The wolf suddenly realized that he was in big trouble because his mean, ruthless and rapacious look had been changed overnight into a look of worry, fear, and dread.

But because he was still as heartless as ever, he decided that he would have to adopt some stratagems to explain the new frightened look on his face. So when he went to his office and all the other creatures saw the new expression on his face and asked him what was wrong, he answered in a very grave manner, "I have just received a message that DOOMSDAY is approaching the area and it will soon be upon us!"

Much to the wolf's surprise the other creatures were not in the least affected by his forecast of doom, but were instead strangely jubilant. For the change in the expression on the wolf's face from total rapacity to pure fear and dread served to release them from their fear of him. This enraged the wolf so that he screamed at them, "I am all wolf and a yard wide and I say that DOOMSDAY is upon us...why oh why do you not feel fear?"

None of the creatures could answer the wolf, and they went around with happy looks on their faces, all chatting together in a most friendly manner. At this the wolf felt the clutch of doom in the place where his heart should have been ... and he finally understood their happiness at his terror as he dropped into the emptiness of death.

Moral: Give wolves a wide berth ... but throw your party when they die.

The Bear Who Made Big Ones

Once there was a bear who dumped in the woods. Though this was not at all unusual, because all bears dump in the woods, this bear dumped on all the trails and bosky dells where the other creatures walked and disported themselves. The bear would dump, stand back, study it, rearrange it with a stick according to aesthetic principles, and then go on his way muttering under his breath things about form, space, and dynamic symmetry.

The other creatures tried to be understanding, thinking that this might be only a passing phase, but then the bear made larger dumps in some of the nicest parts of the woods. Finally they became exercised about it, and they began to complain to the bear.

"You gotta stop dumping where we walk and disport," they all shouted at him. "You have no right to poop up other people's lives!"

At this criticism the bear became very incensed and confounded them all by saying that he was a sculptor of great originality and they were too stupid to appreciate real art.

"You people are so stupid, you don't even know great art when you step in it," roared the bear. "You're nothing but a bunch of Philistines!"

This outburst quite astounded the creatures and they did not know how to answer the bear because they were not at all sure about what art really was. The bear seemed so convinced that his dumps were aesthetic creations that they felt that there was a slim possibility he could be right. So they stood there silently until an old moose who had been listening at the back of the crowd came forward and asked to be heard.

"My friends," said the moose, "what the bear says about our not being able to understand his artistic creations may well be true. I for one confess to being ignorant of art. But rather than continue having strife over this bear's creations, and possibly loosing his artistic legacy for future generations, I make you all the following suggestions: That we set aside a special place of honor for the bear's works, a place where he may work without being disturbed by the common herd, a place where all his works can be preserved and displayed for all those who wish to come and contemplate their message."

The creatures all saw the wisdom of the moose's suggestion, and they agreed that this was a fine decision. The bear himself was extremely flattered. A committee was formed to select a suitable site. They finally chose a fine hilltop, far downwind and away from the trails and bosky dells frequented by the common folk. The bear transported all of his works there and lived among his creations for the remainder of his life. And the creatures returned to their enjoyment of nature. Occasionally they would chance to think of the bear's art...that it was so beyond them . . . so lofty, and so far away from their ordinary lives. And of course the old moose rose to great eminence among them, and was regarded as an authority on things abstruse.

Moral: No matter how high you pile it, culture is not for everybody.

The Dingo's Wife

Away in the outback of Australia, there lived a dingo whose wife was driving him crazy. She would never listen to what he said. When he finished talking, she would say, "Well, I know that," or "That's not what you said last week." Whenever he complained about her not listening, she would change the subject by saying, "I don't know how you can expect me to live like this, why can't we have nice things like other people?" It went along that way till the dingo thought he was going nuts.

Most of the time he only wanted to tell her about things he'd seen while he was out hunting supper for her. He thought the outback was beautiful and everything that happened there wonderfully interesting. But his wife didn't enjoy what they had or where they lived. One day it came to a head.

"When I was up on the ridge this evening, I saw the most beautiful sunset," said the dingo.

"I didn't hear you," said his wife.

"But you were looking right at me when I was talking," said the dingo. "How can you say you didn't hear me?"

"Don't raise your voice to me," said the lady dingo. "Why are you always getting angry over nothing?"

"But it <u>was</u> something," said the dingo, "and it was really pretty!"

"I can't see anything so important in what you see," said Mrs. D. "Everybody <u>sees</u> things, but they don't carry on about them the way you do."

"But it was something special," said the dingo, feeling like he was going crazy, "something terrifically beautiful."

"I don't see anything beautiful in this awful outback," said the dingo's wife. "To me it's all ugly, ugly, ugly, and I hate it, hate it, hate it. And what's more . . . I want to move!"

"Move?" asked the dingo, "move to where? This is where dingoes are supposed to live. This is the most beautiful place there is. It's so beautiful I never want to leave it!"

"Why don't you ever let me have what I want just once? Besides, you promised me we would move."

"All I ever said was that I'd like to live up there on the ridge where we could see the sunrise and the sunset. I never meant move out of the outback, or away!" cried the dingo.

"You said move," replied Mrs. Dingo, "and move means move!"

"Where to," asked the dingo holding his head.

"To where it's nicer," answered his wife.

"Where is nicer?" cried the exasperated dingo.

"I'll tell you where's nicer," said his wife. "It's much nicer in the upfront! I want to move to Sydney! To Civilization!"

At the mention of civilization the dingo's mind finally snapped, and his wife had to phone for the kangaroos in the white coats to cart him away to an institution. Upon being told that her husband would never recover his reason, the dingo's wife moved from the outback to the upfront in Sydney. There she opened a boarding house where she heard every single bit of gossip that was told for ever afterward. But strange to say, her husband made a miraculous recovery and moved even further into the outback!

Moral: Beauty best speaks in silence.

The Superior Donkey

There was a donkey who would always preface everything he said with the words, "In my considered opinion . . ." Even when he was at a party where everyone was having a jolly carefree time, he would speak with extreme gravity and try to have the last word on every subject. As soon as any creature started to say something, the donkey would immediately disagree and point out the flaws in their logic. But the most irritating thing he did was to quickly slip in the punch lines of any jokes they told (whether he knew them or not). Still when he began to lose all his friends, he could not for the life of him understand why.

"I guess that it's just that I am such a frightfully significant sort of person," the donkey would say to himself. "My luster puts them off, and this disorients them and makes them feel envious. They're probably pained by their feelings of inferiority!"

Of course these answers to the problem of his loss of friends satisfied the donkey, but as time went on, he would wake in the morning and feel lonely. After a time, being a resourceful creature, he decided that he must try to seek out more suitable friendships, he would search for superior creatures like himself. Then he hit upon an ingenious idea: He would start a NEWSLETTER in which he would expound all his most brilliant theories on every imaginable subject. And this would attract all of the superior minds in the country!

Shortly thereafter, in a few weeks, the donkey delivered his first edition to all of the newsstands in the country. He called it **The Superior Person's Own Newsletter,** and it featured articles he had written on news of the day, politics, sports, foreign affairs, art, music, and literature. In it he announced that there would be a "Letters to the Editor" section where readers could express their opinions of his articles.

The first issue appeared to be a raving success, and all of the copies were sold out in no time at all. The donkey was overjoyed to learn that his periodical had reached every superior person in the country. But his joy was short-lived for soon the letters to the editor began pouring in. And ... all of the letters from all of the superior people in the country disagreed with absolutely everything he said! Some of them called him an outright idiot. Others called him stupid, commonplace, vapid, unoriginal, contrived, out-of-date, misinformed, wrong-headed, reactionary, conservative, pinko, liberal, bleeding heart, trite, glib, shallow, and much much more. The worst letter of all was one that called him "decidedly inferior."

After that last, although the donkey's psyche was bordering on paralysis, he managed to rally. "I shall stand back," he said to himself, "I shall be cool, and I shall reserve judgement in the fashion of a truly, truly superior person."

Several weeks later after having calmly thought it all over, the donkey came to his final conclusion: "It has become obvious," he said to himself, "that none of these creatures ... not one of them. . . .can comprehend true superiority. I must face the final fact: Loneliness is the curse of the truly superior being!"

Moral: And stubborn consistency is the major fault of all true jackasses.

The Gnu
Who Wanted Fame

Once there was a gnu who wanted to rise from the anonymity of the vast herd and become a movie star. He wanted this because whenever he was introduced to someone, that creature would usually say, "Gnu who?" or sometimes simply, "oo . . ." This always left the gnu feeling diminished, and he would go home and do his acting lessons, and practice singing with his beautiful baritone voice, all the harder.

"I'll show them all someday," he would say.

The gnu's big chance finally came when his agent, a Norway Rat, called to say that he'd arranged a screen test for him with the Big Toad who was the head producer at Cosmic studios. The agent told the gnu, "There is a star part coming up in a major musical that is exactly right for your character type of personality."

On the day of the test, the gnu appeared before the cameras and everything went perfectly, his acting and singing were superb. The following week his agent the Norway Rat called to say that the Big Toad wanted to sign him for the picture and they should meet him the following day to discuss the details of his contract.

The gnu and his agent showed up at the studio at the appointed hour and were shown in to the office of the Big Toad. He gave them both cigars and told the gnu that he'd never seen a better screen test or heard a better baritone voice.

"You've got the male lead in my new musical, kid, and you'll be starring with none other than Sylvia Swan. And all the musical numbers will be backed up with the famous tap dancing Ganders from Flanders. This is going to be a soko-smash production. We are paying you what your agent has asked for and we're giving you an ironclad contract. But there are just three things we're asking in return," said the Big Toad.

"I'll do absolutely anything you ask because this is my big chance," said the gnu, "and I want to make good in the very worst way."

"OK," said the Big Toad, "first off, and no offense, we want you to get a nose-job because your kind of schnozz is just not right for the camera. Second, as long as you're in the hospital and have the plastic surgeon handy, we'd like you to have those clunky horns removed so that we can replace them with a set of something with more upswing. . . you know what I mean, the noble ones that look like tree branches. How's about it kid, you still game?"

"No sacrifice is too great if I can see my name in lights," answered the gnu.

"That brings us to the final little thing we're asking of you," said the Big Toad. "We'd like you to change your name."

"To what?" asked the gnu.

"To Mr. Moose," answered the Big Toad.

The gnu agreed to this final request and went on to become a big star. He had a big mansion, a big yacht, several big expensive cars, and lots of pretty gazelles. But whenever his phone would ring and someone would ask to speak to Mr. Moose, without thinking he would always find himself saying, "Mr. Whoo?"

Moral: Certain kinds of fame are not much different than anonymity.

The Great Gorilla
Catastrophist

Among the intellectual elite of a thriving jungle community there lived a Great Gorilla who espoused a theory of creation through cosmic catastrophe. This gorilla was huge and powerful, but he was also very good natured and clumsy. His house, and laboratory that was supported on stilts, sat under a great Bayabong tree.

One day the gorilla invited a number of his philosopher friends to come and have tea and hear about his new theory. "My thesis is that we were all created in a gigantic cosmic catastrophe," said the gorilla. "Every single thing that happens in the universe is governed by the function of the <u>Resonance of the Great Collision of Primal Cosmic Forces.</u>" But as he said this, he forcefully pounded the table for emphasis, and he pounded it so hard that it sent a heavy bronze vase off the table so that it went flying out the window to bounce off the head of a passing buffalo making a loud "bong."

The buffalo, who was notoriously short tempered, spun around as soon as he was hit seeking the person who had so heinously attacked him. And there was an innocent hippopotamus who was idly scratching his itchy hide on one of the foundation posts of the gorilla's establishment. Thinking that it had been the hippo who had clouted him with the bronze vase, the buffalo struck the hippo a tremendous wallop, a wallop so hard that it caused the hippo to crash into the stilts that supported the laboratory. This, in turn, brought the whole structure crashing down in a heap . . . gorilla, philosophers and all of the scientific equipment! The philosophers all struggled to their feet in a daze, but the gorilla, totally undaunted by the collapse of his establishment, continued to expound his theory.

"There you are!" the gorilla declaimed excitedly. "Living

proof of the verity of my thesis! A perfect demonstration of the principles of the resonance of the primal catastrophe. The blow of my fist hitting the table was transmitted to the stilts supporting this structure. The force was then transmitted to the earth itself, creating that loud "bong" we heard. The waves of force then traveled to the center of the earth . . . Unleashing, I say, the resonances of the primal catastrophe that have lain there for eons sequestered by the forces of gravity. The resonating forces of the primal catastrophe then reverberated back to the earth's surface with such violence as to cause the earthquake that toppled my laboratory and felled this innocent passerby."

The philosophers and the dazed hippo all nodded their heads to the plausibility of the gorilla's cogent reasoning, and they stood around marveling at his theoretical genius. But in the meantime, the angry buffalo perceiving that the gorilla had been the real cause of his getting the knock on the head, swung a round-house punch that gave the gorilla a wallop that knocked him on his keister. The buffalo then stalked off for the rest of the day to rest in his wallow, but the gorilla was by no means through!

"There you have it, the final proof !" shouted the gorilla, "the missing biological effects of the basic catastrophic reverberations! Everyone knows that certain creatures are deranged by earthquakes! And now We know why . . . **The Primal Resonance!"**

The final pieces of the riddle of the cosmic primal catastrophe had fallen into place in the gorilla's theory, and it was soon published under the title The Big Bong Theory of Cosmic Origins. It was hailed as a work of genius throughout the land.

Moral: Theories are often self-portraits of theoreticians.

The Discontented Hen

A hen who thought that roosters had it better in life than hens sat on her roost and brooded about the inequality of it all. She gathered the other hens around her on the roost that evening and gave them all a lecture on how hard it was being a hen and how easy it was to be a rooster.

"The way they strut around the barnyard all day going cock-a-doodle-do!" said the hen, "gives me the poops. They lounge around all day and have an easy life of it while <u>we</u> do all the <u>real</u> work scratching up worms, laying eggs, hatching chicks! Ever see a rooster tending chicks? Oh my, no. Mr. Rooster is too busy strutting around the barnyard, and chasing innocent hens!"

Some of the other hens disagreed and said they thought that roosters had their place, and added that they <u>were</u> pretty stylish in their dress and musical in their crowing.

"Ha," said the hen, "crowing indeed! You'd crow too if you didn't have to poop out an egg everyday of your life! We scratch for food from morning till night to get up the strength to lay eggs while your Mr. Rooster is out gallivanting the whole night. Then they have the gall to go out in the barnyard and make a racket at four in the morning that wakes us all out of a sound sleep. That's some hard life! Some soft existence!"

At this point in her diatribe she became so agitated that she had to flap her wings to regain her balance on the roost. "I'd just like to see one of <u>them</u> try to lay an egg. I'll bet you <u>he</u> wouldn't be strutting around for a few days after <u>that</u>! No sirree bob! Laying an egg takes all the starch out of a body for the rest of the day and most of the night! Feeding chicks is no picnic either. It's scratch, scratch, for all the worms you can find, and never a 'please' or 'thank you' from the little rascals. And do they ever come to visit old mom after they've grown up? Ha! Old mom doesn't come in for diddly-doo from her grown up chicks! Here's us hens out scratching our claws to the bone to earn our feed while a couple of lazy roosters live on easy street!"

Finally, an older hen interrupted her discontented colleague and said, "Biddy, no one knows better than I that we hens don't have an easy time of it, but I think that our lot isn't all that bad compared with the prospects of roosters."

"Why, how you talk," replied the discontented hen, "those roosters are living in a veritable paradise!"

"It may seem that way," answered the old hen, "but did you ever wonder just why there are so many of us hens and so few roosters? You know as well as I do that there are as many roosters born as there are hens."

"I suppose they're off somewhere having a good time . . . if I know my roosters," replied the discontented hen, "but just where that might be I've never figured out. They just seem to disappear after a while."

"The reason they disappear," said the old hen, "is that they get turned into fried chicken!"

Hearing this shocking news, all of the hens tucked their heads under their wings, said their prayers, and went to sleep. And the discontented hen never complained of her lot again.

Moral: Understanding the other fellow's lot is the first step to equality.

The Down-And-Out Crows

Three down-and-out crows carrying shopping bags perched on the crosstrees of a telephone pole.

"Terible day," said the first crow.

"I've seen worse," said the second.

"A bad-luck day," said the third, "and I've never knowed anything but bad luck."

"I could tell you a thing or two about bad luck," said the first crow. "I'm your original bad-luck bird."

"That may be," said the second crow, "but I could tell you guys about hard times that would make you think you'd lived your lives in a corncrib."

The three crows argued back and forth about who was the unluckiest. They finally decided each would tell his story and then they would take a vote on who had the hardest life. The first crow began with the history of his misfortunes . . .

"I was born in a nest in an old dead tree on the poorest farm in Arkansas," he said. "The land was so dry that the corn wouldn't grow and the worms was all dead, so I was raised on boll weevils and sawdust. They call me the 'Hard-Times Kid!'"

"I gotta admit that's a sad tale," said the second crow, "but you was fortunate that you knowed your parents. I was raised an orphan on accounta my folks being shotgunned by a farmer on the day I was borned. Second day of my life I fell out of the nest and was almost ate by a cat, but I managed to waddle into the brush in the nick of time and save myself. I raised myself up in the brush on a diet of ants, bugs, and stump water. I was three years old before I managed to teach myself how to fly, but because of my early misfortunes its been bugs and stump water for me ever since. The taste of corn gives me the fantods."

The third crow sighed at the conclusion of the second crow's story. "Oh how I envy those brung up genteel," he said. "My poor egg was pitched out of the nest by cowbirds before I was hatched, and I never knowed parents or home. If it hadn'ta been for my egg falling into some rotten leaves, I'da never made it into this cruel life. The heat from the rotten leaves hatched my egg, and I grew up not knowing who or what I was. All I ever had to eat was leaf mold and mushrooms. For years I though I might be a potata bug, but only last year I crawled out of the leaf pile to discover I was one of the bird family. I still don't rightly know just what kinda bird I am, but all I can say is that I hope like hell I ain't a crow, because you two are the biggest damn liars I ever seen in my life!"

The first and second crow had to admit that the third crow was the unluckiest of the three, so the three of them broke open their shopping bags and shared their corn together. When they had finished, they folded their shopping bags neatly, tucked them into their pockets, and flew off to steal some more.

Moral: Competition . . . stimulates enterprise.

The King Of The Baboons

The people of a country populated by baboons selected their king every ten years by holding a pissing contest by the leaders of the nation. The winner would hold the office for ten years, but could extend his tenure if he could win the contest for the next term against all contestants. At the time of this story there lived a king of the baboons who had ruled the land for two terms. As his second term of office drew to a close, the king who was wise and just, became fearful because the two leading contenders for the kingship were both unmitigated rogues. But they were also great pissers known throughout the land. He therefore decided to enter the contest once more, though he was far beyond his prime.

"The old king won't even clear the end of his shoes, much less reach the twenty foot mark," some of the more irreverent baboons jeered. "Somebody should tell the old putz that this is a pissing contest and not a dribbling meet," they laughed.

Despite the criticism, the old king persisted in his intentions, and when the day of the contest arrived, he showed up with the two rowdy contenders at the Tree of National Decision where the contest was traditionally held. As he stood surveying the scene, the king saw that the two contenders appeared to be even bigger scoundrels than he had previously believed, and this made him doubly determined to retain his kingship. So just before the contest began, he stepped forward and addressed the judges . . . .

"Honored judges," said the old king, "I am well along in years and have grown somewhat forgetful. So may I ask that you recite the rules of our competition for all to hear?"

The judges decided to humor the old king as he had been a great favorite and well loved by the people. So the judge with the loudest voice complied. "The rules of the contest are as follows: The contestant is to place one hand on the Tree of National Decision. . . and then make his play. Distance of play is measured from where the hand touches the trunk of the tree to the greatest length of play. Greatest distance wins."

The first contender was a truculent baboon of enormous size. This bully swaggered to the tree trunk, whipped out his organ and made a play that achieved a length of twenty-one feet! This was a new record and the crowd went absolutely wild!

The second contender then stepped forward. This was a baboon of huge dimensions in every respect, and with the sneering countenance of a blusterer and a beer guzzler. Touching the Tree of National Decision, he gave a mighty heave and made an amazing play of twenty-three feet! At this the crowd burst into a sustained roar, and the populace seemed confident that they had found their new leader. But then the old king stepped forward and an embarrassed hush fell over the crowd as they sensed the coming humiliation of the old worn-out baboon.

But, grabbing the trunk of the Tree of National Decision, the old king vaulted upward and pulled himself to the top of the tree. There, while holding to the trunk with one arm, he released his old and once mighty spout, and made his play while shouting down to the judges . . . "From where the hand touches the trunk of the Tree of National Decision to the greatest distance achieved! I say, Bring on your measuring line!"

And the judges had to comply because the old king had played by the rules as spoken. The distance of his play, accounted for by its longer arc, was <u>forty feet</u>!

Of course, the old king retained his kingship, and he ruled his land and subjects with wisdom and justice for another ten years. And his last reign was considered the golden age of Baboon civilization.

Moral: Politics is a game not always played to best effect on the level.

The Camel Who Became
A Prophet Of Love

Once there was an orphaned camel who was raised by a wicked stepmother, an old Dromedary who treated him with cruelty and contempt. His days were spent carrying loads of sticks or doing other lowly chores. But his nights were passed sitting by the campfires hearing the salty tales of the old camels, and listening to their hauntingly plaintive desert love songs.

One day the little camel addressed the wicked stepmother thus, "Stepmother, can you tell me why the old camels are always singing love songs around the campfire at night? And why are they always talking about humping?"

Turning on the innocent little camel with a shrewish curse, the wicked stepmother snarled, "Hush your filthy mouth you little wretch! There are certain things that decent camels such as myself just don't talk about!" And with that, she gave the little camel such a smack on the chops that she traumatized him forever.

This act of traumatization had two serious and irreversible effects on the poor little camel. First, it led him to an obsessive interest in love songs, and it was not long till he had memorized the words to all the current hits. Then he memorized the standards, and then even the oldies! He soon became a popular singer around the campfires at night. This in turn led to the young female camels following him and making goo-goo eyes, and then screaming at the top of their lungs when he sang his songs.

The second irreversible effect of the traumatization occurred when he learned the definition of humping from some of the more rowdy members of the caravan. This information led to his developing a serious obsession with humping, which worked out quite nicely, because his singing obsession easily provided the females for his humping fixation.

Things went on quite well for the young camel for a brief time, but the elders of the caravan soon objected to his behavior. "Your behavior is objectionable," they shouted at the young camel. "It is also salacious, concupiscent, and overtly libidinous! Since you obviously can't conform to the standards of this family-oriented caravan, and do not respect our conservative approach to the humping question . . . Consider yourself cursed of Allah, and no longer a member of our entourage."

The young camel became angry at what he felt was jealousy of his singing and humping successes. He shouted back at them in a bold baritone voice, "If Allah had not intended us for humping, he never would have given us humps!"

So the young camel set out across the vast expanse of desert to wander in meditation. But he was followed by a large number of the young females who had become addicted to his singing voice. His meditations eventually resulted in his seeing visions of a new and more melodious existence. These same visions then led him to form a new religious sect which he called, "The Pathway of the True Humpers." The creed was that of your standard paradise on earth: natural foods were stressed, lots of singing, but the almost continuous humping was the core part of the belief system. The sect settled in a secluded mountain valley that was difficult of access from the outside world, and far from all the caravan routes. Nothing was heard of the sect again until a hundred years later when a new breed of camel suddenly appeared . . . that had two humps.

Moral: Allah always finds ways to explain his truths to unbelievers.

The Obituary Notice
Of A Fastidious Cockroach

He was one of the better sort, a true gentleroach, liked by all, envied by few, he will be mourned by many, for he was, above all things, a self-made roach. And though he was eminently successful, his true greatness lay before him.

Reverses in his family's fortune led to his being born into the relative poverty of a one-star restaurant. But by the end of his life he had reestablished his family's eminence in the culinary field by sheer hard work, and by the astute exercise of his considerable charm and talent.

In early life his family sacrificed much to send him to one of the better schools. He then went on to win a scholarship to the university where he worked nights in the kitchens to supplement his meager income. He graduated cum laude in food science.

Legendary as an athlete of superb abilities, he held the world record for the three yard-dash for several years. His ceiling free-falls are still spoken of with awe in university athletic circles. He also had an avocational love of spelunking that brought him recognition for his icy nerve and reckless daring in tight situations.

Upon graduating from the university, he entered the produce business where he soon became a dominant figure. He prospered to such a degree that he was able to establish his entire family in the three-star restaurant that was to remain the family residence for the remainder of his life.

He was a member of all the better clubs. The Gourmet Society was the center of his greatest activity (he sat on the board of directors). As a leading gourmet, he was known for his discriminating tastes in the foods of all nations, though he particularly favored the French Cuisine. He was also a flawless judge of vintages. And among the members of the society, he is remembered as a marvelous raconteur as well as being a dinner companion that was always much sought after by all the discriminating hostesses of the day.

Most notable of his personal traits was his fastidious concern with good grooming. His sartorial bearing was flawless, always elegant and correct, with never so much as a hair out of place. But it was, in fact, the matter of grooming that led to his untimely demise. He loved his daily tub, and it was during his ablutions last Thursday, that he made an unfortunate slip into a bowl of boiling consomme. Despite all the efforts of the rescue squad to pull him from the frothing inferno by forming a living chain, the rescue effort had to be abandoned because of the hellish temperature of the liquid. Strange to say, he had a serious brush with death two years ago in a narrow escape from a garbage compactor.

Our hearts all grieve for our sterling friend. He will be lovingly remembered by his grieving parents, by his 132,750 sisters, his 134,221 brothers, and his 2,078,034 cousins. The exact number of his wives and children is still being calculated, and should be published sometime next week.

Interdenominational services will be held at sunrise on the pastry cart. The eulogy will be delivered by the president of the Gourmet Society.

Moral: Class always tells.

The Old Sow
Who Foretold The Future

An old sow who had raised many litters of piglets was beset by the depressed feeling that her usefulness was over. Then one day she had a vision in which she saw two smoked hams, some bacon, and a pile of sausage.

"I have had a vision of the future," she said to her friends that evening. "I have seen the specter of foreshadowing doom!" And saying no more she sank into a deep and silent brooding, with an otherworldly look so solemn that it shocked her friends to the core.

"The old sow is having visions of the future," said her friends to all of the other creatures. "She just sits in her wallow all day and looks out into somewhere that nobody else can see!"

Most of the animals avoided the old sow after that and didn't go near the wallow if they could help it. But one day all of that changed.

It seems that a cow who had been feeling poorly discussed her condition with her friend the ewe, "I've just been feeling so odd lately! I have the lurking feeling that something awful is going to happen, but I don't know what. Do you suppose that the old sow could tell me what my future holds? I'd give a pretty penny to know what's bothering me," so she decided to go down to the wallow and tell the old sow all about it. The old sow was glad to see the cow because she'd been feeling lonely and useless, but she didn't say anything until the cow had told her all her problems. Then, when the cow had finished, the old sow looked off into the distance and said in a creepy voice, "Those who eat grass shall prosper."

Now this wasn't much, but the cow felt suddenly relieved. She went right home and told everyone that the old sow was a genuine seer. Later, she took the old sow a basket of apples as a gesture of gratitude.

A few days later all of the animals were surprised to see a sign down by the hog wallow that read:

PSYCHIC READINGS BY THE OLD SOW
CONTRIBUTIONS ACCEPTED

After this all of the animals began to consult the old sow whenever they had a problem or felt out of sorts. To those who ate grasses and vegetables, she gave flattering and hopeful readings, but to meat eaters, she always had something somber to say like, "He who lives by fang and claw shall know the wrath of chronic indigestion," or anything else that sounded ominous enough to steer them toward a low protein diet. They all brought her generous contributions of food stuffs so that the old sow ended up living pretty high off the clairvoyance. This improved her own state of mind considerably.

All went very well for the old sow until one day, in the midst of her prosperity, she had another vision. This time the vision was of mountains of fruits and vegetables and pies and cakes. She really loved this vision and she held on to it all day long as she wallowed in the mud. But at the end of the day the vision had worked a surprising effect on her, it had so totally altered the expression on her face that she had completely lost the haunted and far away look that had served her so well as a clairvoyant. After this happened, because of the change in her appearance, her business as a psychic reader went to pot . . . she was just too damned cheerful looking! So she was forced to go back to rooting for tubers and acorns. However, by that time, she was too old and tough to be turned into hams or sausage.

Moral: Dame fortune is a wicked slut . . .but oddly fair.

The World's Serious Beastball Game

One day an armadillo walking down the street encountered a lion and a tiger. The two were wearing striped shirts, white shorts, and little beany caps. The armadillo first felt apprehension, but this feeling disappeared because they both smiled broadly at him and greeted him like old and trusted friends.

"Why, just the very fellow we've been lookin' for," said the tiger to the lion. "Just notice the steely look in this fellow's eye."

"Tough customer if ever I saw one," replied the lion. "A tangle with me, count your lumps later type!"

The Armadillo, who had always sought a macho image, squinted his eyes and said in his gruffest voice, "Howdy gents."

"What did I tell you, What Did I Tell You?" said the Tiger. "You can see it in the way he carries his shoulders! Oh, he'll do, He'll do!"

"Da'st we ask him?" responded the lion. "This ain't the kinda jasper you wanta rub the wrong way!"

"Let's chance it," said the Tiger.

By this time the armadillo was bursting to know just what this was all about and was very eager to please the two sports. "Anything I can do fer you fellers?" he asked.

"Well pardner," the lion answered, "We're in big trouble because us lions and tigers are holding a friendly little game of ball and the star player ain't showed up."

"I'm real sorry to hear that," said the armadillo in his gruffest voice.

"From the minute we saw you," said the tiger, "we knowed that you could handle his spot. How's about helping out?"

"Betcher boots," answered the armadillo. "What position?"

"Why, the most important one of all," responded the lion. "You'll be a sort of roving center, always in the thick of the action!"

"That's for me," said the armadillo.

So the lion and the tiger escorted the armadillo to a big stadium where there was a sign that read:

LIONS VS TIGERS

WORLD'S SERIOUS BEASTBALL

TODAY!

When they appeared on the field there was great cheering. Then a gorilla wearing a black and white vertically striped shirt with white pants came and took the armadillo to the center of the field and blew his whistle. The next thing the armadillo saw was a bunch of lions running at him from one side, while a bunch of tigers were bearing down at him from the other. In total panic, he curled himself up into a tight ball, and for the next two hours, he felt himself being rolled, bounced, kicked into the air, and banged into posts.

When all the action was over, the armadillo uncurled himself to see that the lions were carrying one of their members around the field on their shoulders, while the tigers were off to one side of the field glowering and arguing with the gorilla in the striped shirt. So the armadillo finished uncurling himself and quietly scuttled off the field unnoticed by anyone. And when he arrived safe at home at last, he congratulated himself on having the good sense to have not played ball with such a violent bunch of maniacs.

Moral: Without a ball there can be no ball game.

The Land
Of The Jackals

An orangutan who was a famous explorer and single-handed sailor once sailed his ship into the harbor of the Land of the Jackals. There at the principle quay he was met by the jackal Minister of International Friendship and Goodwill.

"Welcome to you pilgrim!" said the Minister with a broad smile. "I am here to acquaint you with our customs and to serve as your guide to our principle points of interest. We will begin our tour with a visit to our Temple of Hospitality where you will be given food and drink at the most moderate rates."

"Wonderful," said the orangutan, "I am both parched and famished."

On the way to the Temple of Hospitality, the Minister described the jackals' political system and philosophy to the traveler. "We are a simple people," he said, "and we believe in two simple attributes . . . freedom and generosity! Our two political parties reflect these beliefs in that they each support one of them. We have the Freedom Party and the Generosity Party, and the two parties alternate tenures of office.

"I adore simplicity," said the orangutan, "and I've always believed in the perfectibility of animal nature!"

"Here we have attained it!" said the Minister of the jackals as they arrived at the door to the Temple of Hospitality."

Once inside the Temple, they were seated at a table where they were shown the menu from which they both ordered many delectable sounding dishes. Soon after they ordered, their table was surrounded by a crowd of friendly jackals who chatted away about freedom and generosity until the food arrived and the minister and the traveler prepared to dine. But just as the traveler was about to put the first bite of food into his mouth, he felt a tap on his shoulder. Turning around he found that there was no one there. When he turned back to the table he found that every morsel of his food was gone. The traveling orangutan was amazed.

"There you have your first glimpse of one of our major tenets!" said the jackal Minister. "Freedom ... in one of its most delightful and spontaneous manifestations!"

"But that was my food," wailed the angry orangutan.

"Precisely!," replied the jackal Minister. "Which has afforded you the wonderful opportunity to display our second most valued quality ... Open hearted generosity!"

The orangutan indignantly called the waiter for the bill, but he was dismayed to find that his pocket had been picked and he was unable to pay the outrageous charges for the food and the jackals hospitality. When it was discovered that he was broke, the Minister of International Friendship and Goodwill immediately summoned the police and the orangutan was hustled back to the harbor and put on his boat. "There are certain types we just don't allow in our wonderful land," he said as he stalked angrily away.

When the orangutan was safely aboard his ship, he found that the sails, rigging, compass, and engine had been removed as a harbor and dockage fee. All that was left was a pair of oars, which he immediately put to use so that by sundown, the Land of the Jackals was but a dot on the horizon.

Moral: Freedom and generosity are universally accepted virtues, but always count your change.

The Sisters Of
The Dismal Swamp

A razorback sow who had been crossed in love was advised to take council from the Sisters of the Dismal Swamp on the night of the full moon.

"He left me for another," said the sow, "and I 'd like to fix his bacon for him!"

"Can do," said Sister Bat (who represented air).

"But it'll take some doin'," said Sister Toad (who represented water).

"We'll brew up a potion on him," said Sister Snake (who represented earth).

So the three sisters gathered up the ingredients and set a big kettle to boil over a pile of sticks as the moon rose high above the cypress trees. At midnight they began to invoke the spirits with the following incantations:

Sister Bat:
" Gnats and skeeters, mites and flies,
sting his ears and blind his eyes!
Air pollution, factory stench,
choke the lungs of heartless wench!
Lizard's gizzard, eye of newt . . .
now they won't behave so cute!
Creatures of the air and night
help this brew to come out right!"

Sister toad:
" Rats and weevils, worms and glue,
equals are in this here stew.
Talents small enlarge by hype,
mixed with slimly slugs and tripe.

Make all that's fair become what's foul,
confound the brain, and twist the bowel!
Cold disdain, conceited smirk . . .
handmaidens in our social work.

Sister Snake:
" Lurch and slither, shuffle, trudge,
add a dollop crankcase sludge,
castor beans and milkweed goo,
skunk cabbage . . . just a leaf or two . . .
dingle berries, tumble bug,
sweepings from beneath the rug.
We sisters never want nor waste . . .
add a bit of salt to taste!"

All:
Creatures of the dismal swamp,
come around our fires and romp,
slither, fly to us, or shamble,
hop, or do the muskrat ramble . . .
tonight's the night for whoop-dee-doo,
come share the Sister's crawdad stew!"

After the Sisters had shared their brew with all the
creatures of the Dismal Swamp, the razorback sow politely
thanked them for their efforts on her behalf. She then returned
to life in the community with a greater faith in the future and a
new outlook. Her new sense of self-esteem enabled her to form
a more suitable relationship, and this in turn enabled her to
open her own crawdad stew franchise which soon prospered.
Her former lover vanished without a trace.

Moral: Seek professional help . . . and let the good times roll!

The Two Fleas

Two fleas, one inept and the other deft, had been comrades since childhood, sharing good times and bad. But one day the deft flea told his friend the inept flea that he was leaving for the big city to make his fortune.

"Take me along," the inept flea pleaded. "You're my buddy, I hate to see you go."

"He travels the fastest who travels alone," said the deft flea. "Face it, you're a klutz and its time for us to part."

The inept flea felt sad and betrayed and slowly went back to the crowded subdivision on the sheep dog where he lived. For a long time he sorrowed for his lost friend, but after a while the sheep dog had pups and the inept flea was able to move on to one of the females and start a new life. He became the real estate agent for the dog's territories and by hard work managed to get ahead. Later, When <u>that</u> dog had pups, the flea was able to branch out into new territories, and by dint of hard work he eventually became one of the leading fleas in the real estate business.

Then one day, who should show up but his old comrade, looking the worse for wear and asking for a handout.

"Why is it," asked the inept flea, "that I who have always been inept and a klutz am now a regular tycoon, while you who have always been considered deft are now a failure and a bum?"

The deft flea looked at his old friend with a tear in his eye and said, "I hate to burden you with the story of my downfall, but if you've got a minute or two, I can give you a rundown on the low points."

"Shoot," said the inept tycoon, "but try to make it snappy because I gotta lunch appointment on an Airedale and I gotta look over some new properties after."

"It all started when I got into the wrong company," said the deft flea. "It was racing dogs. I lived the fast life for a while, but then I got onto a looser . . . ended up at the pound. There was a real bad crowd there. After that it was mixed breeds, and then I fell to the lowest . . . cats! I've even been on mice and hamsters!" Shame and humiliation showed on his face.

"Look old buddy," said the inept flea, "you may be a looser and a bum, but you're still my old pal. And if you're looking for a quiet place to settle down, I got just the spot. It ain't nothing grand, mind you. It's in a depressed area on an old bloodhound. You interested?"

"You bet pal," said the deft flea.

"OK," said the inept tycoon, "You'll have this place rent-free, and you'll be a sort of caretaker. What you do is, when you get to the bloodhound, go up the left front leg and follow the trail all the way to the spine, turn right and go all the way back till you get to the tail. At the base of the tail, turn right for half an inch then left for an inch and a half. The property on the left will be your territory. There's about three square inches of wild country there, but its yours old buddy . . . for the sake of old times!"

Moral: It's not how far you travel in life . . . it's how you read the terrain.

The First-Rate Rat

Once there was a son born to a poor family of rats who lived in the basement of a vegetable market in a run-down neighborhood. The family subsisted on carrot tops, old cabbage leaves, and rotten oranges, but the poor couple wanted their only son to rise above these disadvantages and make his mark in the world.

"Don't be a dummy like me," said the father. "Get yourself an education. My parents died when I was young and I had to go to work early long before I woulda graduated. But you gotta get that old diploma! You gotta study your numbers and get ahead!"

So the young rat went to school and studied all the teachers' numbers, learning what pleased or angered them. He said what they said, did what they asked at all times, always looked interested, and never disagreed. His grades were always at the top of his class. And he got so good at getting the numbers of his teachers that he soon began getting the numbers of fellow students who were soon sharing their lunches with him. After a time his father asked him how it was going.

"OK, pop," said the young rat, "I've learned all about getting numbers and am pretty good at it,"

"Numbers are important," said his father. "Once you know your numbers you're on you way, but you also gotta work hard at being a winner!"

That seemed reasonable to the young rat, so he went back to school and started practicing to be a winner. Realizing that winning meant getting somewhere first, he discovered that the best way to that end was to find shortcuts. So he found all the shortcuts around the school and was soon the winner in all of the contests and competitions. But one day he was caught taking a shortcut and was accused of cheating. So he went home to his father and told him that he had been caught taking a shortcut and that winning didn't always bring success.

"Winning don't mean a thing," said his father, "if you don't have the reputation of being a good citizen!"

That made sense to the young rat, so he went back to school and worked on evading consequences, shifting blame, and always appearing respectable and honest. A year later he went home to his father and told him that he'd won the Good-Citizen of the Year award.

"Well, sonny," said his proud father, "there's just one more thing you gotta learn, and that's how to recognize opportunity when you see it!"

With that the eager young rat returned to school once more. He learned how to recognize the achievements of others and how to take the credit for himself. He was soon regarded as being super-creative and was given his diploma with all possible honors. The students and faculty cheered him as he was given his sheepskin. His father was very proud of his outstanding son.

Upon leaving school, he entered the business world, and after a very few years and some brilliant moves managed to become an owner. In a few more years, he was enormously wealthy and owned homes in various cities. But by that time he had put both his parents into a nursing home and never came to visit them. A few years later, after he had accumulated a huge fortune, he became a respected philanthropist who gave generously to all the charities and causes. He was awarded the Rat of the Century Medal. He died respected by all and had the largest funeral ever seen in the city.

Moral: Some rats are born . . . some are made . . . while some . . .

The Grizzly
Dream House

A grizzly bear who had married the girl of his dreams decided to build a dream house for his bride.

"The past is where all the mistakes were made!" said the bear. "The world of tomorrow is where it's at. We're gonna be bears of the future honey pie. I'm gonna build you a modern home with ultra-modern design, and all the labor saving conveniences."

"Anything you say, sugar," said his bride, "but before you start, I'm gonna give you a great big smooch!"

So after the smooch, the bear got out his drawing instruments and designed their dream house by following all the latest architectural ideas and incorporating all the latest technological advances. When he had finished his drawing, he showed it to his bride to find out how she liked it.

"Looks OK to me sweetie buns," she told him, "but how's about giving your tootsie a big smackeroo?"

When the exchange of smackeroos was over, the grizzly bear went out to buy a lot, purchase building materials, and construct their new house. This took considerable time.

But when the new house was finally finished, all of the neighbors were amazed to see the squares, triangles, and circles in glass, steel, concrete, and plastic. "That's some modrun house!" said one neighbor. "What the heck, it's a free country!" said another, while one asked, "What do you suppose it means?" But the grizzly was very proud of his house and was the happiest bear in the world when he carried his bride through the sliding glass picture window.

"Where's the threshold, babykins?" his bride asked him. "I always did so want a threshold!"

"This is a modern house, inkypinky," said the grizzly. "Modern houses only have sliding glass picture windows."

"Where's all the furniture and rugs snookums?" asked the bride, "and why is it all so bare?"

"Less is more," replied the grizzly. "What we do is sit on those cubes and those plastic balloons tweetietwoo. What say you an' me do some fancy bear huggin'?"

"I can't do any huggin' if I don't feel cozy," said his bride. "I always wanted a cozy nest."

The grizzly tried to pacify his bride by mixing her a drink from the chemistry bar, turning on the stereo-video, starting the house cleaning machinery, offering to let her play games on the computer, and promising he would install their own personal atomic reactor to save on the electricity bills. But all this was to no avail, and his bride sulked.

"I don't want to be a bear of the future anymore," said his bride. "All I ever wanted was to be comfy . . . and modern isn't comfy . . . modern is un-comfy!"

So the bear quickly sold his dream house to some upwardly mobile hyenas and bought an old cave on a hill side that overlooked a green valley. On the day they moved in, the bear and his bride sat on an old sofa that looked out of the cave mouth and admired the sunset together.

"How's about a little razzmatazz?" said the grizzly.

"You're talking my language." said his wife.

Moral: Less is less . . . always has been, always will be.

The Fabulous
Old Goat

There was an old goat who had tried everything possible to make a buck to no avail. Finally he seemed to be looking down at the bottom of the barrel, when his wife, who was completely fed up, shouted at him.

"You've lost all of our money, my fur coat, and your very shirt on that fraudulent gold mine stock, and every other lousy idea" she yelled at him. "When I tell you we need to find an nest egg ... what do you do? You come up with another hare-brained idea."

"Well, we almost had it with that chicken farm," the goat replied, "and I've never known a nicer bunch of chickens. They'd do anything for me, give me the feathers right off their backs!"

"A swell bunch of freeloaders," the nanny goat replied.

"Well, the hotdog stand did alright for awhile, didn't it?" asked the goat.

"Just like the used-cart lot, the jazz band, and the organic turnip patch," said the nanny. "Now we happen to be really up the creek."

"But we've still got our health," answered the goat hopefully.

"Not for long if you don't shake your tail and bring us in some moola," snapped the nanny.

His wife's complaints finally got the old goat's goat, so he went for a walk to think over the possibilities and consider his past mistakes. A couple hours later he returned home to his wife with a great big eager smile on his face.

"I <u>know</u> that look!" his wife said, "that is the look that tells me you've got another wild hair up the old kazoo. What's it gonna be this time ... a spaghetti tree, a lead into gold mine, a tap dancing school for one-legged sailors, a soda fountain-of-youth? All I want is a little geetus, a little spondulicks, a little gold laid by for a nest egg!"

"This is it baby! Our golden nest egg!" enthused the old billy goat. "I've figured out the way to turn all of my past mistakes into cash."

"OK, Mr. Wise guy," answered the nanny goat. "You just tell me how anyone can capitalize on years of gloom, disaster, and total failure."

"Simple," said the old goat, "I'll put all of my years of rich personal experience into literature . . . I'll write fables!"

"What in the hell do you know about fables," sniffed his wife contemptuously.

"What's really to know?" responded the old goat. "All I know is that fables make you see the ridiculous things in disastrous situations. And I happen to know disaster backwards and forwards."

"You can say that again," responded the nanny.

So the old goat set about writing fables about his strange encounters with all of the freaky creatures he had met in his years of business failures. After six months or so he had a nice batch of them ready for publication. So he took them to a goose who was known as a big publisher. The goose promised to call the old goat within a week to let him know whether his fables were publishable. However, a month went by and the goat had heard nothing from the goose. But he was undaunted by this silence and thought that it might be the thing to do if he dropped in at the gooses' publishing house to find out the fate of his fables. Several hours later he returned home with a big smile on his face.

"How goes it Aesop," said his wife with a cynical smile. "Are you still in the fable business? Let's see the golden nest egg!"

"That silly old Goose lost my manuscript," answered the goat.

"Idiot!" screamed his wife, "why are you smiling like a loon? What's so blasted funny about that. It's just another disaster in a long train of disasters."

"It gave me a great idea for a new fable," chortled the delirious old goat. "I'll call it . . . 'The Goose That Mislaid The Golden . . .'"

He had to quickly duck a frying pan his wife hurled at him, and he ran out the back door and retreated to an old hen house left over from his chicken farming days. But as he entered the hen house he was suddenly struck with a new idea out of the blue . . . a Perpetual Motion Device that would run on . . . a big eager smile came over his face as he got down to work.

Moral: Optimism gives heart to all enterprise . . . and it don't cost nothin'.

The Giraffe Who Finally Rose To Eminence

A giraffe who was one of those perpetual university students who can never make up their mind on a specialty, finally had to consider gainful employment after he had frittered away the last of his inheritance. In desperation the giraffe sought the guidance of a cassowary who was a famous university Don known for his wisdom.

"What particular field do you find the most interesting, the most exciting, the most fascinating?" asked the sage old cassowary.

"Well, to tell the truth, I've studied just about everything, but I can't actually <u>do</u> anything," answered the giraffe. "I'm really stumped."

"That suggests to me that you would do wonderfully well in either an executive or an advisory position," intoned the cassowary, as he profoundly ruffled his plumage.

"That sounds absolutely wonderful," said the giraffe, "I've never been one to hammer and saw, spruce things up, or till the soil. I'm sure there must be something for me in the telling-what-to-do or not-to-do line! If you think that really suits my personality."

"From what I see of your personality," replied the cassowary, "you are fatuous, insipid, disdainful, superior, condescending, and indecisive. All of which would fit you for an executive position <u>except</u> for the trait of indecisiveness. That seems to narrow it down to something in the advisory field. Have you ever considered the practice of law?"

"I'm not at all sure about that," said the giraffe, "I'd hate like stink to advise someone to do something that turned out to be improper or illegal. I might end up being criticized or disbarred or sued myself."

"Well," responded the cassowary, "if you don't mind my commenting on your personal appearance, there is something both lofty and supercilious about your appearance that definitely strikes a note of untouchable self-righteousness . . . with a dash of superior knowledge. It's a look that says you could not be expected to speak the common tongue."

"How very perceptive of you!" exclaimed the giraffe.

"I've got it!' cried the cassowary, "The healing arts! You have the very bearing and attitude of a great healer!"

"Do you really think so?" whinnied the excited giraffe.

"No doubt about it," answered the cassowary. "The beauty part of it is that all you will ever have to say is . . . 'Things are progressing as well as can be expected' or 'We must wait and see' or 'We have done all that can be done and it is now in the hands of God.' Actually there are about ten phrases that can carry you through almost any situation that may arise." And here the cassowary looked at the giraffe for his approval.

"Love it," said the giraffe.

And so the giraffe entered the field of the healing arts, where, because of his lofty and superior look, he was soon recognized as one of the leading practitioners. And soon, because of his stature and haughty bearing, he was always pointed out as a most promising and rising figure at the meetings and conventions of the healing societies to which he belonged. His patients adored his remote bedside manner, as it suggested that his mind was far off in the realms of science. He soon grew rich on referrals. And as he grew even richer, he was regarded with even greater respect. In time he rose to highest eminence in his profession.

Moral: Guard your health . . . with your life.

The Altruistic Alligator

Way down in the Okefenokee swamp there was an impressionable alligator who became a convert to a sect of altruists that was led by an escaped circus rhinoceros. The philosophy of the rhino involved vegetarianism, songs of interspecies understanding, the conversion of non-believers, and the generous support of the evangelist through healthy tithing.

"Practice sensitivity to others," the rhino instructed the converted alligator. "Love all creatures regardless of their repulsiveness or edibility, observe strict vegetarianism, smoke or drink no stimulants, give generously to the sect, and above all else, smile a happy smile and give a heartfelt greeting to all potential converts."

From that day forward, the alligator lived by the strict code of his adopted belief: He rose at dawn, did 30 minutes of calisthenics, practiced smiling before the mirror for an additional 15 minutes, had a light breakfast of fruits and nuts, and then went off to work in the handbag factory. His spare time was devoted to converting unbelievers through door-to-door preaching of the philosophy of altruism. The alligator was given his own special section of the town to convert.

By a strange twist of fate, the alligator was allotted an area of town inhabited mainly by middle class rabbits who were notoriously lacking in interspecies fellowship. This served as a spur to the alligator's religious zeal, and was a challenge to his new-found philosophy of altruism. The alligator would walk up to a door, knock vigorously, then as the door opened, he would smile his broadest smile and say,

"Why hello there neighbor, I'm bringing you a message of love, vegetarianism, interspecies understanding, and . . ." But by that time, the rabbit would usually scream and slam the door, while any loose youngsters running about the yard would head for the bushes. This always left the alligator smiling broadly on the front porch and wondering what he had done wrong.

"I think I may have to work on my smile a bit more," he'd say to himself. "Somehow my altruism is just not getting through to these rabbits!"

Then he would go home and practice his smiling technique before the mirror, and saying "Well hello there ma'am," or "How ya doin fella?" till he was blue in the face. But however much he practiced or varied his method of smiling and greeting, he continued to receive the same negative response. In fact, if possible, things got worse.

The rabbit community was terrified of the visiting alligator, that's all there was to it. They attempted to have him legally barred from canvassing, but that failed because the civil rights animals found that he was an altruist in good standing. So the rabbits simply stayed behind locked doors, and the alligator was forced to shout his altruism at them from the front porch, which terrified them even further.

After a while, the strain of his constantly rejected altruism began to affect the alligator's health. And he grew very thin on the vegetable diet and became hypersensitive to slights. Finally, the alligator woke one night from a nightmare in which he dreamed he was gorging himself on a platter of fried rabbit.

The following morning the alligator resigned from the altruist sect, quit his job at the handbag factory, and returned to his native swamp. He never thought of vegetarianism again, but often when he was sitting by his campfire at night roasting a plump rabbit, he would break out into a song of love and interspecies understanding.

Moral: Whenever an altruist smiles . . . count his teeth and run for the bushes.

The Turtle Society
For Universal Excellence

A select group of intellectual, scientific, and artistic turtles approached a wealthy elephant to gain his support for their project to found a Society For Universal Excellence.

"We desire to encourage only the very best in all fields of endeavor," said the aged turtle they had elected as their spokesperson.

"That seems a very laudable undertaking," responded the elephant.

"Laudability is the very essence of our organization," replied the old turtle. "We hope to establish the canons of laudability in every field of animal creation."

"Just how do you intend to go about establishing this laudability?" queried the philanthropist.

"We shall begin the process," answered the spokesman turtle, "with a formal announcement in the press that a Society For Universal Excellence has been formed for the purpose of encouraging the highest achievements in all the higher realms of endeavor. We will make it known that our purpose is to do honor to all those who have reached the pinnacle of accomplishment. We will also include a list of the founding members ... you will, of course, be mentioned as the principle sponsor."

"But in what way do you actually bestow the laudability?" asked the philanthropic elephant.

"We will begin, of course, by awarding Gold Medals and Certificates of Merit to all of the founding members," answered the old turtle. "And once we have done this, we can begin to search out laudability amongst the common folk."

This gave the elephant pause, and he asked, "But what criteria do you use to determine what is, or what is not, laudable."

To this the old turtle quickly replied, "We base our considered judgement on our own firmly established canons of laudability. They are founded on the bedrock principles of our own certified, Gold Medal-winning achievements in our various fields of endeavor."

The elephant pondered this for a while, and then said, "But what if some creature comes out of left field, so to speak, and does something very good that is not at all understood or appreciated by your Gold Medal-winning members?"

"We believe," responded the turtle quickly, "that one of the first principles of laudability is to not rock the boat. After all, society must have established standards and values or surely chaos and anarchy will rule!"

"But what if this hypothetical non-member does something that wins over the hearts and minds of the common people, and it's based on some newly discovered principle not yet understood by your group of Gold Medal-winning experts?" asked the elephant.

"That poses a difficult problem," replied the turtle, "but since it is we who must determine what is officially laudable, we can simply ignore, or where necessary, isolate the offender of official laudability . . . or, that failing, we will discredit the wretch. But if those measures fail, we can simply wait until the offender dies and then posthumously celebrate his genius as being representative of our own highest standards!"

The elephant frowned at this and said, "I do not think that this is altogether laudable. I am afraid that I cannot support your efforts."

But despite the wealthy elephant's rejection of their proposed society, the turtles quickly obtained the support of a group of super-rich hyenas, and the Turtle Society For Universal Excellence went on to determine the standards of excellence in animal society for many years thereafter.

Moral: True excellence always shines with its own light.

The Duck Who
Spoke The Truth

There once was a duck who would not go, "quack, quack, quack." Instead he only spoke what he felt to be the truth, and he soon became disenchanted with the other ducks around him.

The other ducks would greet him by saying, "Hiyafella, howyadoin, howtheyhangin, howsawifenkids. Quack, quack, quack."

The truthful little duck replied,
"I'm feeling lousy, I'm not doing very well, they're not hanging, and I'm not married. What's more, I don't intend to ever get married until I can find a girl who doesn't go, 'quack, quack, quack,' all the time!"

"You're gonna sleep cold for a long, long time," laughed the other ducks, "quack, quack, quack."

"There's gotta be somebody around who thinks real thoughts and says real things instead of just quacking platitudes," answered the truthful duck. Maybe I can at least find a friend who doesn't go 'quack, quack, quack' to everything I say."

"Lotsaluck!" quacked the other ducks, "quack, quack, quack."

The truthful duck continued to always say what he felt to be the truth, and he kept on looking for another duck that did the same. Then one day he encountered a beautiful girl duck swimming in the middle of the pond.

Maybe this will be the duck of my dreams he thought and he said, "Hello, Miss, I'd like to introduce myself and get acquainted with you. Would you consider sharing your thoughts and feelings with me?"

"Oh wow," said the girl duck, "how groovy! You are really weird and outasight . . . quack, quack, quack."

The truthful duck was saddened by this. "I guess beauty of form doesn't necessarily mean beauty of spirit," he thought as he sadly swam away.

Shortly after this he happened to encounter a fine looking mallard swimming along the edge of the pond.

"How do you do sir," said the truthful duck, "I see that you're examining the rare aquatic growth that can only be found in this particular area of the shoreline. I happen to be very interested in botany myself."

"What are you . . . some kinda fag?" answered the mallard. If you must know, I'm thinkin' about the big game next Thursday between the Pintails and the Canvasbacks. The Backs are goin' to cream them Pintail pansies . . . quack, quack, quack."

The truthful duck swam away feeling ever more depressed and wondering if he might be some sort of biological aberration because he was devoted to the truth. "I must be the misfit!" he sighed to himself. Then he encountered a plain looking girl duck, swimming along in a dejected manner. Her expression of woeful sadness made him think of the bright future he had always imagined.

"Hey there," he said, "the world isn't all that bad."

"Yes it is," replied the girl duck, "if all you ever hear anyone say is, 'quack, quack, quack.'"

"That," replied the truthful duck, "is a very penetrating observation. I've found the same thing to be almost universally true. But I'd like to hear more about your thoughts and feelings about life. How about the two of us swimming along together for a while. Hey. . . that's a truly beautiful smile you've got there. It sort of lights up the whole world! If you don't mind my saying so." . . . She didn't mind at all. And so the two truthful ducks lived happily ever after. But once in a while they would look at one another and go, 'quack, quack, quack', just for the hell of it.

Moral: Hang in there . . . keep looking . . . there is someone out there for you!

The Ant Who
Challenged Destiny

Once upon a time an ant of singular qualities was born into a colony of busy and industrious ants. As he grew to adulthood, the little ant yearned to better the conditions of his teeming fellows and advance his race.

One night the little ant had a vision of amazing grandeur, and from this vision he conceived the idea of painting heroic murals in the vast corridors of the anthill. So he worked out his plans and took his designs to the leaders of the ant colony.

"This is very distracting," said the old general who was the chief leader of the ants. "What's it supposed to mean?"

The little ant responded with enthusiasm, "It depicts, sir, the whole evolutionary striving of the ant race. It represents our yearnings, and our potentialities for future greatness!"

"Bosh!" said the general, I see nothing here of marching, soldiering, or milking aphids. Why, if we let you put up these here muriels, it'll slow up production, and we'll have trouble on our hands before you know it!"

So the committee of leaders rejected the little ant's plans to enrich their society with great art. But the little ant did not lose heart! He was determined to find the means to turn these leaders from being cultural boobs, to ants of great cultural responsibility. So he decided to write a book that would show the philosophical roots of the cultural potentialities of the race of ants. And after several years of labor, the little ant completed his work and brought the first volume to the committee of leaders.

When they had finished reading a few pages of the book they called the little ant into the council chamber. The little ant looked eagerly at the chief leader, and the old general said, "You've managed to give us all headaches. As far as we can see, you're still trying to talk us in to putting up those muriels in the halls. We're getting sick of this propaganda kiddo, you better shape up or we'll put your ass in the army. You capiche, buster?"

But the little ant did not agree with the general, and once again he pondered the problem of the stupid leaders of his race. Finally, he arrived at the solution to his problem. So again he labored, until years later he produced a volume of keen psychological insights showing how the ants were emotionally paralyzed because they were conditioned from infancy to work in a mechanized society. When he had finished he took his volume of finely honed reasoning to the leaders.

But again the general and the committee were not impressed. Speaking for all of them the general said in a very stern voice, "You're beginning to be a real pain in the ass kid. You spent this entire boring book trying to insult us leaders, and run down our sacred traditions and bad-mouth our whole immortal civilization!"

But as the leaders berated the little ant and heaped their abuse on him, there came a great deluge that flooded the vast caverns of the ant hill. And all the teeming thousands were lost, save the little ant who swam his way upstream and battled his way through the flooding torrent to the top of the ant hill. There he discovered that the cause of the titanic disaster was an old cow who lazily had relieved the pressure of her bladder on the ant hill. . . dooming the entire civilization with her thoughtless act of bladder relief, and never once realizing the havoc she had wrought on a race of her fellow creatures.

As the valiant little ant sat drying himself in the warm evening wind, he began to laugh with a resonance that reached out to the evening star and the rising constellations. And from the heavens, there seemed to echo back a voice that said, "Well done little ant, you have given your best . . . now go build your civilization anew!"

So the little ant went forth on the following day to seek others of his kind to help him build a new and better life. He found other ants, some dispossessed by war, accident and survivors of the great flood, as well as wanderers, outcasts, and misfits. And he formed them into a loyal band with his visions of a new civilization that would honor beauty and equity. They soon found a site on which to begin their enterprise.

They began excavations for tunnels and chambers of the little ant's design. The work started well, but in time it grew more difficult as some of the misfits and outcasts began to disrupt the work. This forced the little ant to form a group of policemen ants to help him keep order in the expanding system of tunnels and caverns.

All continued to go as planned until a group of the more subversive types organized squads of resistance against the former little ant, who was now called 'First Leader' by all the those working on the new civilization. The dissident ants worked to disrupt the food supply and to undermine the building of the tunnels, which set the rank and file workers into panic. This forced the First Leader to organize his police into a constabulary with squads of specialists to deal with the anti-social elements. This solved the problem and the construction went ahead very quickly and was completed ahead of schedule. With the completion of the tunnel complex the ant population suddenly expanded at a very rapid rate and soon the food supply was inadequate to feed the swelling numbers and a food shortage threatened the population.

Again First Leader stepped in to solve the problem by building huge dairy caverns to house an industry of aphid farms. Prosperity finally arrived at the new ant civilization to such a degree that it became the envy of all the other ant civilizations in the general area. Some of the civilizations seethed with jealousy.

Then in the middle of one summer night, without any warning at all, the new ant civilization was invaded by a savage army of ants from afar who were bent on plundering the wealth of this new civilization. The streets of the caverns seethed with the raping and pillaging soldiers of the enemy. Many lives were lost before the brave First Leader was able to rally his followers and fight off the invaders.

After this great 'Patriotic War To End All Wars' as it was called in the press, there was no alternative but for the First Leader to form a permanent standing army. The First Leader went about this task with great vigor, and in a short time, the new civilization lived in peace and security under the protection of its standing army. The Ant formerly known as First Leader, was now known as First General, and he felt that his mission to build a new society had finally been achieved.

Many years of prosperity followed. Then one day as the aging First General sat with his assistant leaders in the council chamber, there came to them a young ant seeking an audience with a strangely familiar light of enthusiasm in his eye. The audience was granted, and the young ant presented them with an elaborate set of plans for decorating the corridors and caverns of the ant civilization with elaborate bas-relief sculptures showing the evolutionary striving of the ant race. The First General, who found the designs for the bas-reliefs oddly disturbing, was quick to respond.

"This is the most hare-brained set of designs I've ever seen since the dawn of this entire civilization!" he bellowed. And calling the sergeant of the guard, he yelled, "Get this nut out of here and put him to work in the maintenance department! IMMEDIATELY!"

Moral: Life is short . . . and art is long . . . but usually not long enough.

The Musk Ox
And The Glory Hole

Way up in the frozen northland there was a musk ox who lived the life of a prospector. He had never had much luck, but he hung on hoping that someday he'd strike it rich and maybe find a 'Glory Hole' (that's a place in a stream where a whole lot of gold sinks into one spot). Each spring, after the thaw had set in, he'd go down to Dawson and spend what few nuggets he'd found for strong waters, some hilarity, and a bit of female companionship. But this time, at the Satin Slipper Saloon, he finally met a beautiful dancing girl named Buffalo Annie.

"Why yore just the purtiest Buffalo Gal I ever dun met," said the musk ox. "Yu have just plumb stole muh heart right out from under muh ribs! How's about yu and me goin' out dancin' by the light of the moon?"

Buffalo Annie, quite taken aback by the strong musky odor of the stranger, could only respond, "Whooo-oof!, when's the last time you had a bath pardner?"

The musk ox, who felt somewhat rebuffed by her frank remark, was quick to reply, "Why all of us musk ox's smell like this Miss Annie! Yu see when yu live up in the frozen north like we do, without no neighbors for a hundred miles in every direction, our musky smell travels out on the winds and all of the other musk ox's know that we're keeping in touch. It's a kinder tellygraph system of the nose yu might say."

"Well I surely do get the message," sniffed Buffalo Annie with raised nostrils. Then, looking at the small size of the musk oxen's poke that held only the few nuggets he'd found during the year, she sniffed again and said, "I'm just solid booked up for the rest of the evening Mr. Ox, and come to think of it . . . for the next month . . . an probably for the next year! So if you'll please excuse me, I gotta heavy date with the nearest winder. Whooooo-weeeee!"

The musk ox was heartbroken by Buffalo Annie's obvious rejection. So he left the saloon, bought his next year's supplies, and headed on back to the frozen north to continue his prospecting, and living his lonely existence. But a few months later his luck changed for the better (as luck sometimes will), when on the stream he was prospecting . . . he struck a Glory Hole! The glory hole contained enough gold nuggets to make the musk ox rich for life! So with joy beating in his shaggy breast, he soon packed his gold nuggets and returned to Dawson to find his one true love.

Of course the news of the musk oxen's strike spread through the town like a prairie fire as soon as he got there. And that night, dressed up in new duds, the musk ox showed up at the Satin Slipper Saloon where he was enthusiastically greeted by all the assembled miners, and by none other than Buffalo Annie herself.

"Where you been keepin' yerself hansome . . . long time no see!" said Buffalo Annie in her most husky, seductive drawl. Then, with her eye on his now bulging poke, she did a little shimmy and a little shake and said, "How's about you and me doin' some fancy steppin' out by the light of the moon Musky?"

So with his big heart fairly thumping in his massive chest, the musk ox replied, "I'd be right proud to cut a caper with ya under the moon Miss Annie!"

Then as the two of them danced to a rag-time rigadoon by the light of the full moon, Buffalo Annie sighed her most tender and seductive sigh and said, "Wheeeee-ooooo, that is some wonderful masculine scent yer wearin' there musky! It really separates the bulls from the steers . . . sorta sweeps a girl straight off her feet. Ya know musky, I could see right off that you're my kinda guy. Why dancin' with you just plum takes my breath away!"

So the musk ox and Buffalo Annie reached a very tender understanding that night. And soon after that . . . they were married and lived happily ever after.

Moral: In some circumstances it is better to be stinking rich . . . than it is to be stinking poor.

AFTERWORD

To my fellow members and residents of the human zoo... It is my hope that we <u>human animals</u> all recognize that we share the susceptibility to these traits of character.

Go in peace.